Volcanoes

By Leslie Dinaberg

The Child's World
www.childsworld.com

The
Child's World

Published in the United States of America by The Child's World®
P.O. Box 326 • Chanhassen, MN 55317-0326
800-599-READ • www.childsworld.com

A big thanks to Koss and Zak, for keeping the eruptions to a
minimum when I was working on this project.

ACKNOWLEDGMENTS

The Child's World®: Mary Berendes, Publishing Director

Produced by Shoreline Publishing Group LLC
President / Editorial Director: James Buckley, Jr.
Designer: Tom Carling, carlingdesign.com
Cover Art: Slimfilms
Copy Editor: Beth Adelman

Photo Credits
Cover—Getty Images/National Geographic (4)
Interior—AP/Wide World: 17, 22; Corbis: 5, 6, 11, 18, 19;
Getty Images: 9, 12, 26; iStock: 15, 21, 24, 25; Photos.com: 8, 14, 28.

LIBRARY OF CONGRESS CATALOGING-IN-PUBLICATION DATA

Dinaberg, Leslie.
  Volcanoes / by Leslie Dinaberg.
     p. cm. — (Boys rock!)
  Includes bibliographical references and index.
  ISBN 1-59296-739-6 (library reinforced : alk. paper)
  1. Volcanoes—Juvenile literature. 2. Volcanic eruptions—
Juvenile literature. I. Title. II. Series.
  QE521.3.D55 2006
  551.21—dc22

                       2006004599

CONTENTS

WHAT IS A Volcano?

Underneath its rocky skin, the earth is is a very hot place—hot enough to melt rock! Sometimes the melted rock works it way farther and farther upward—all the way to the earth's surface. Volcanoes are places where the liquid rock comes out, or **erupts**, at the surface. The most familiar kinds of volcanoes look like mountains with a hole on top. The hole is called a **crater**.

The hot liquid rock is called **magma** when it's deep underground. It's called **lava** when it reaches the earth's surface. Some volcanic eruptions are amazing to see—and dangerous!

About 50 or 60 volcanoes around the world are active. That means they still might have lava flowing out of

them, either now or in the future. Some of them are ones that erupt all the time, like Hawai'i's Mauna Loa (mau-nah loh-ah) and Kīlauea (KEE-lau-way-ah).

After an eruption, the lava cools and hardens into solid rock. In fact, much of the earth's surface is made up of cooled volcanic rock, including the sea floor, many islands, and lots of other land areas. Long ago, hot gases from erupting volcanoes also helped form the earth's **atmosphere**.

Japan's famous Mount Fuji is a stratovolcano. It's 12,388 feet (3,776 m) tall.

Here are some of the different types of volcanoes: *Stratovolcanoes* are the most common type. They're cone-shaped mountains built of lava, ash, and other materials that sometimes erupt from the top. *Cinder cones* are made up of loose rock pieces called "cinders." Cinder cones usually erupt only once, for perhaps a few years. *Shield volcanoes* are rounded volcanic mountains formed from thin, fast-moving lava that flows out often. Hawai'i's famous Mauna Loa is an example. *Domes* form from the slow build-up of thick, oozing lava. California's Lassen Peak is an unusually large volcanic dome.

In 1943, a volcanic eruption in a Mexican cornfield formed the world's best-known cinder cone, Paricutín.

In North America, volcanoes are found mainly in Hawai'i, and on the West Coast from California north to Alaska. You don't have to be standing next to a volcano to be in danger if it erupts. Hurtling rocks, choking ash and dust, and other dangers can cause problems many miles away.

Ring of Fire

The lands bordering the Pacific Ocean, mostly north of the equator, are home to many of the world's volcanoes. On a map, these lands form a circle, sometimes nicknamed the "Ring of Fire," after the fiery heat of all those volcanoes.

Yikes! That's hot! In Hawai'i, this well-covered volcanologist carefully carries a sample of red-hot lava.

Scientists called **volcanologists** study volcanoes. Wearing special protective gear, they sometimes go within feet of **molten** hot lava!

2

HOW ERUPTIONS Work

Earth is made up of three layers—the crust, the **mantle**, and the core. We live on the rocky outside layer, or crust. The crust isn't one solid piece. Instead, it's made up of huge pieces or *plates* that slide around on the mantle below. They don't move fast—just a few inches per year. Deep under the crust, the rock sometimes melts and forms magma. The magma is lighter than the rock around it and starts to rise. Sometimes it goes all the way to the surface and erupts. Most eruptions—and volcanoes—are along the edges of the crust's plates.

This drawing shows the inside of a volcano. Magma works it way up through the earth's crust before erupting as lava.

Volcanoes erupt in different ways. Some eruptions are explosive, blasting lava, rock, ash, and gases high into the air. Others aren't explosive at all. Instead, the lava flows out slowly.

Scientists use the Volcanic Explosivity Index (VEI) to say how big an eruption is.

They give each eruption a number from 0 (gentle) to 8 (enormous!). Nobody's actually seen an eruption as big as an 8, but there are signs that they happened long ago.

This enormous blast of rock, ash, and smoke was probably a 4 or 5 on the VEI.

Most of the volcanic eruptions during the past 10,000 years have had VEI numbers of 3 or less.

In 1982, an airplane nearly crashed because ash from an eruption clogged its engines. Since then, airplanes are not allowed to fly over active volcanoes!

Erupting volcanoes can be very dangerous! Sometimes superhot, superfast clouds of gas, ash, and dust zoom down a volcano's sides at over 100 miles (161 km) per hour. Lava flows move more slowly but destroy everything in their way. Hot volcanic gases can poison the air, and ash and choking dust can cover everything. Sometimes volcanoes cause earthquakes, mudslides, and other hazards, too.

Sometimes a volcano erupts for months or years. On the

Caribbean island of Montserrat (MON-sahr-raht), the Soufriere (SOO-free-air) Hills volcano has been erupting since 1995. Two-thirds of the island is now unfit for people to live. Thousands of people have had to leave their homes.

Ash from the Soufriere Hills volcano has covered this car and house on Montserrat.

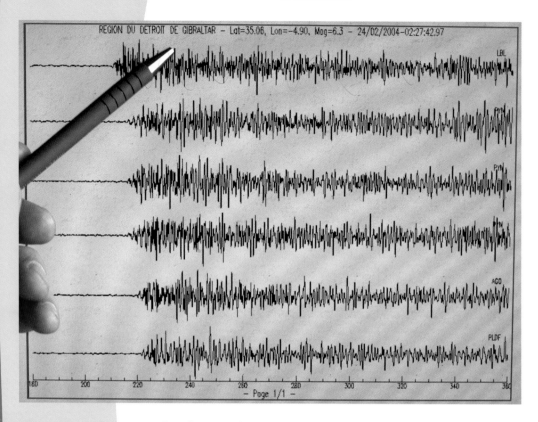
REGION DU DETROIT DE GIBRALTAR - Lat=35.06, Lon=-4.90, Mag=6.3 - 24/02/2004-02:27:42.97

LBL

PY

AGO

PLDF

180   200   220   240   260   280   300   320   340   360
— Page 1/1 —

The jagged lines on this seismometer show where and how much a section of the earth moved.

Scientists use special tools to try to tell when a volcano will erupt. A **seismometer** (size-MAH-meh-ter) measures movement in the ground. If the ground is moving a lot, it could be a sign that the volcano might erupt at any time. That still doesn't tell scientists when it will happen, though.

Other signs of a possible eruption are small lava flows, increased heat in the ground, or the release of some types of gas.

Volcanologists study volcanoes to look for signs of upcoming eruptions. Knowing when an eruption will happen can help save lives.

One of the most famous eruptions happened in Italy almost 2,000 years ago. In A.D. 79, Mount Vesuvius erupted suddenly, burying the nearby town of Pompeii in ash. Most of the people got away, but some died and were covered with ash. The ash protected, or **preserved**, the town for hundreds of years. Uncovering the town has revealed a lot about life at that time.

In the 1960s, scientists were working at the site of an ancient city in Turkey. They

Ash from the eruption of Vesuvius preserved the town of Pompeii almost perfectly. This photo shows statues, a walkway, and parts of some buildings. They're almost exactly the same as they were long ago.

found a painting that might show an erupting volcano (most likely a nearby stratovolcano called Mount Hasan). If so, it's the earliest painting of a volcano ever found—about 8,000 years old!

RECORD
Breakers

The worst eruption in the history of the United States was Mount St. Helens, in Washington State. Scientists knew the volcano would erupt someday—they just didn't know when.

On May 18, 1980, the whole north side of the mountain exploded! Although many people had left the area, 58 people were killed by the blast. The explosion flattened trees, killed thousands of animals, and caused $1.2 billion in damage.

OPPOSITE PAGE
Smoke poured from the top of Mount St. Helens for months after 1980's huge eruption.

The biggest volcanic eruption in modern times was in Tambora, Indonesia, in 1815. The eruption created an enormous amount of volcanic ash. Mount St. Helens created only about one-hundredth as much!

Lava flows can go on for miles. Sometimes the lava cools quickly on top but is still red-hot underneath. This red-hot lava flow is in Hawai'i.

Today, the world's most active volcano is Kīlauea in Hawai'i. This volcano has been erupting since 1983.

Hot and cold: Mount Etna in Italy is hot inside, but the outside is covered with ice and snow.

The tallest active volcano in Europe is Italy's Mount Etna, and it's very active indeed! Mount Etna has erupted hundreds of times in the last 3,500 years.

The tallest volcano in the world is Ojos del Salado in northern Chile. It's 22,560 feet (6,876 m) tall. The largest volcano in the world is Mauna Loa in Hawai'i.

OPPOSITE PAGE
This drawing from 1888 was based on what people saw when Krakatau erupted.

The loudest volcano eruption was in 1883. When Krakatau (krak-uh-TOW) erupted in Indonesia, people heard the noise almost 3,000 miles (4,828 km) away. They said it sounded like the distant roar of heavy guns and that the roaring continued all through the night.

Many islands are formed by volcanoes that erupt underwater. Below, Molokini in Hawai'i was a volcanic cone that collapsed and filled with water.

Volcanoes create some of nature's most amazing displays. They have the power to destroy, but they are also beautiful. Ash from volcanoes can make soil so plants can grow. Volcanoes also bring diamonds and precious metals, such as silver and gold, to the earth's surface. All this volcanic activity shows us that the earth is alive and changing all the time.

Make Your Own Volcano!

You can make your own volcano by mixing baking soda with vinegar and dishwashing liquid. *Make sure you have an adult help you with this project.*

Place a large plastic bottle in a flat pie pan (or a cookie sheet with sides). Put four tablespoons of baking soda and a tablespoon of soap into the bottle. Add a few drops of red food coloring if you want your "lava" to look real. Then slowly pour in vinegar until the mixture starts bubbling.

Pressure in the bottle builds up as the vinegar, baking soda, and soap mix and make gas bubbles. The gas forces the suds (the lava) up through the bottle. Eventually, the suds will come out of the top and flow over the sides. Stand back and watch your homemade volcano erupt!

GLOSSARY

atmosphere   the mass of air surrounding the earth

crater   a bowl-shaped hole in the ground surface, or at the top of a volcano

erupt   break out of something, as in lava erupting from the earth

lava   liquid rock from within the earth after it has erupted from a volcano

magma   liquid rock while it is still inside the earth

mantle   the layer of the earth located just below the crust, or outer layer

molten   melted by heat

preserved   protected for a long period of time

seismometer   a device that measures the movements within the crust of the earth.

volcanologists   scientists who study volcanoes

FIND OUT MORE

BOOKS

Danger! Volcanoes
by Seymour Simon
(SeaStar Books, New York) 2004
This book by a well-known science author has great photos and lots of facts about volcanoes.

Discover Volcanoes & Earthquakes
by Martin F. J. Flower
(HTS Books, Lincolnwood, IL) 1993
This book has loads of information about the science of volcanoes and earthquakes.

Eyewitness: Volcano & Earthquake
by Susanna Van Rose
(DK Publishing Inc., New York) 2004
Look for fun facts about volcanoes, plus dozens of photos.

Volcanoes
by Michele Ingber Drohan
(PowerKids Press, New York) 1999
This book describes different kinds of volcanoes, where they are, why they erupt, and how people can protect themselves.

WEB SITES

Visit our home page for lots of links about volcanoes around the world: www.childsworld.com/links

Note to Parents, Teachers, and Librarians: We routinely check our Web links to make sure they're safe, active sites—so encourage your readers to check them out!

INDEX

LESLIE DINABERG has more than 14 years of experience as a writer and editor for a variety of magazines, Web sites, and newspapers. When she was in fifth grade, she read every single book in her school's library—but back in those days, there were only a few books about volcanoes!